Virus Attacks Heart

By Shannon Murdoch

For JF. Because it mattered.

Virus Attacks Heart was first produced in May 2014 by Pull Together Productions as part of the Planet Connections Theatre Festivity in New York City. The production was directed by Brian Gillespie with the following cast:

Beatrice   Gina LeMoine
Jamie   Luke Wise

Virus Attacks Heart received its world premiere in November 2014 at Venus Theatre in Laurel, MD. The production was directed by Deborah Randall with the following cast:

Beatrice   Karin Rosnizeck
Jamie   Joe Feldman

Acknowledgements

Special thanks to Deb, Karin, Joe, Brian, Gina, Luke and everyone involved with the Venus Theatre and Planet Connections productions. You took my words and made something spectacular. Thank you will never be enough. Thanks also to Bailey Jordan Koch, Lily Dorment, Keenan Jolliff and the people of EAT New Works Festival in NYC who helped shepherd this play into the world. This play would not have been possible without the love and support of Juliet Lamont, Kim Weinert and Michael Grigg.

Virus Attacks Heart
© Shannon Murdoch
Trade Edition, 2015
ISBN 978-1-63092-082-1

NURTURE by Johnna Adams

Synopsis: Doug and Cheryl are horrible single parents drawn together by their equally horrible daughters. The star-crossed parental units' journey from first meeting to first date, to first time, to first joint parent-teacher meeting, to proposal and more. They attempt to form a modern nuclear family while living in perpetual fear of the fruit of their loins and someone abducting young girls in their town.

Cast Size: 1 Male, 1 Female

CHARACTERS

BEATRICE   37 years old, but looks younger.

JAMIE   19 years old, and looks it.

STAGING
A park bench in a local park surrounded by bushes.

A small bedroom with a double bed. A door to the bathroom. A tall, weathered wardrobe. An open suitcase in one corner. Clothes scattered over the floor.

A single bed in the emergency ward of a small, suburban hospital. A table next to the bed. A plastic chair.

A nightclub in the basement of an industrial building.

NOTE ON STAGING
Settings should be suggested rather than slaves to accuracy to allow for quick transitions between scenes and locations.

VIRUS ATTACKS HEART

SCENE ONE

(The Park Bench. Night. Jamie, dressed in jeans and a t-shirt, stands on the park bench urinating into the bushes. A thick coat lies on the bench beside him.)

JAMIE: Easy. That's the word. Not simple, but easy.

(Beat.)

JAMIE: You can feel words. Did you know that?

(Jamie waits for a response)

JAMIE: You knew that. You've got those eyes and sometimes you don't need words when you've got eyes like you have eyes …

(Beat.)

JAMIE: I don't have eyes like that. So I need words. Need them like sleep. And breath. And company. And I have them. Most of them. One day I'll have all of them. I will. You just watch me. With those eyes of yours.

(A rustling in the bushes right where Jamie is urinating. Jamie abruptly stops.)

JAMIE: You okay there? … Hello?

8

(Beat. Jamie shuffles down the park bench and continues urinating.)

JAMIE: Not simple. No. But easy. You understand the difference don't you? … Most people don't. They'll laugh at you, call you little freak, call you worse. Push you away, get away, get away, get away now, if you try to make them understand the fundamental difference between common words.

(Jamie stops.)

JAMIE: I thought you were one of those people. I did. Just for a minute. Just until … But you're not are you? … Are you? … Hello?

(A rustling in the bushes. Jamie zips his jeans up. He puts his coat on and does up every button.)

JAMIE: Cushy, soft, easy-going, painless. Not plain, uncomplicated or unproblematic … Easy. Not simple.

(The rustling in the bushes stops. Silence. Jamie bounces up and down on the balls of his feet.)

JAMIE: Boom boom shaka shaka boom … Are you still there?

(Silence.)

JAMIE: Boom boom shaka shaka boom … I don't have an iPod. I lied about that. But I'm going to get one. Boom boom shaka shaka boom. Again and again and

... Can you say something?   Just make a noise or ...
Come out. Just come out now and we'll ...

(Jamie jumps down off the park bench.)

JAMIE: Because I'm ...

(Jamie walks to the edge of the bushes.)

JAMIE: ... Hello?

(Jamie walks into the bushes.)

SCENE TWO

(The Bedroom. Night. Beatrice enters, dressed in a short, peasant-style dress and knee-high boots. An enormous handbag is slung over her shoulder. Her hair sticks out wildly, a few twigs and leaves stuck in it. She stops and drops her handbag on the floor.)

BEATRICE: *(calling out)* This is crazy isn't it?

(Beat.)

BEATRICE: *(to herself)* This is crazy … *(calling out)* I'm mostly okay with crazy. Not kill your mother in her sleep because she never let you cut your hair like Cyndi Lauper crazy. But just a little bit off the centre crazy. The dirt path instead of the smooth road crazy. The stay up all night for no reason crazy. The … When for a baby moment the thump thump drang of the world stops and for once your voice sounds like song, crazy.

(Beat.)

BEATRICE: *(calling out)* That's the crazy I meant when I said This is crazy. *(To herself)* Stop saying crazy … *(Calling out)* Could I have some water?

(Beat. Beatrice slowly moves around the room, taking in everything. She picks up a t-shirt from the floor. On the front it has a cartoon lamb spurting blood from a gunshot to the face. On the back it says 'Kill the babies'. Beatrice

11

reads it, thinks about it, and then laughs. She drops the t-shirt back onto the floor and continues walking around. She stops. A moment later, she breaks out into uncontrollable laughter. She loses her balance and falls face first onto the bed. She lays there for a moment before jumping up.)

BEATRICE: *(calling out)* Water! Did I say that? I need to lose some drinks. I'm completely soaked through.

(Beatrice falls back onto the bed and sticks one leg in the air.)

BEATRICE: I said to myself, not tonight. No sweetheart, not tonight.

(Beatrice unzips her boot.)

BEATRICE: But she can't be stopped.

(Beatrice shakes her leg and dislodges the boot from her foot.)

BEATRICE: That beast of a woman.

(Beatrice makes large circles in the air with her leg.)

BEATRICE: All flesh. All muscles. Moving. Left to right. Right to left. And all the places in between.

(Beatrice expertly flicks her left leg and her boot flies across the room. It hits the opposite wall and falls to the floor.)

BEATRICE: All flesh and all muscle.

(Beatrice sits up on the bed, facing away from the door. She dances her hips left to right and right to left. Jamie enters, fully dressed, and stops at the doorway. He watches.)

BEATRICE: Wonderful, isn't she? And awful. And 723 other things, most of which don't have names.

(Beatrice stops, falls back on the bed. Jamie quickly exits before she sees him. Beatrice turns over and sticks her other leg in the air. She unzips her boot and repeats the same action.)

BEATRICE: Inflated, enhanced and completely unbeliev-able. Hot and cruel and breathing sweet sweet air straight to the blood. Everywhere. Everything … Twelve Drink Beatrice.

(Beatrice flicks the boot off. It hits the wall and falls on top of the other boot. Beatrice sits up.)

BEATRICE: *(calling out)* I don't talk like this. This is her … Just so you know.

(Beatrice sniffs her arm, then licks her arm.)

BEATRICE: God, it's coming out of everywhere.

(Beatrice leaps off the bed and does a series of star jumps.)

BEATRICE: Twelve Drink Beatrice is the pinnacle of alcoholic achievement. The gold medal. The Nobel Prize. The meat tray at the local pub.

(Beatrice licks her skin again, pulls a face. She strides around the room, making laps around the bed.)

BEATRICE: I mean, you tell yourself two drinks Beatrice, with that low, rough voice that says these are the rules. These are your boundaries. Don't you dare test me.

(Beatrice stops in front of the wardrobe.)

BEATRICE: But two drinks? Two little, little drinks? Gone in a gulp. Two gulps if you're trying to be lady-like about it. But gone. Gone too soon, and the differences between Two Drink Beatrice and No Drink Beatrice can only be viewed under a pretty hefty microscopic device.

(Beatrice opens the door of the wardrobe. It's empty with a series of drawers on one side and a shelf at the top).

BEATRICE: Little, little, Two Drink Beatrice with her hard thoughts clotting the mind. Little, little stupid I shouldn't have worn this dress. I can't wear this dress. What was I thinking? Jesus. I can feel my arse. I can just feel it being everywhere. And I have nothing to say. I never have anything interesting to say, I don't like me, I like nothing about me, starting and ending with my arse but 723 other things, all of which have names. I need a hole. Just a dark, dark hole. Please don't look at me, please look at me, please do something, because I am little little, stupid stupid Two Drink Beatrice in need of her dark dark hole.

(Beatrice climbs up on the first drawer, loses her grip, and falls back onto the bed. She immediately gets up and starts climbing up the wardrobe. At no point, does she look like she will make it to the top.)

BEATRICE: Enter Four Drink Beatrice. Who promises in a clear soft voice that all thoughts, hard or otherwise, are simple knots flicked straight with the twist of one of her fingers. But Four Drink Beatrice is too much. Nothing but a bitch. A sweet bitch, but the bitch burns too hard for the sweet to ever catch the light.

(Beatrice climbs onto the top drawer. The wardrobe starts to wobble. Beatrice stops and clutches the sides of the wardrobe.)

BEATRICE: Eight Drink Beatrice snarls at Four Drink Beatrice as she smooths the thoughts and almost makes them disappear. Eight Drink Beatrice remembers all the good stories and none of the bad ... But she's grabby. Grab, grab, with nails that cut deep. Right into the lolly sweet centre of the flesh.

(Beatrice starts climbing again. The wardrobe continues to wobble.)

BEATRICE: She needs you. Close. Too close, and she'll grab and dig and grab and dig until you have to physically restrain yourself from slapping her seven ways from Sunday. It's all heading towards disaster, faster than seems possible. The words come too furious. More, more, each one more chiselled than the last. Words that so swiftly, so effortlessly, become an unwieldy axe, slammed right into your face ... So there's nothing to do. Nothing to save the moment ...

(Beatrice climbs up to the top of the wardrobe and lies on top of it, holding on for dear life.)

BEATRICE: Except ...

(Beatrice slowly, precariously, rises to a crouching position on top of the wardrobe.)

BEATRICE: Here she comes. Do you see her? Swacking her hips and flashing the flesh.

(Beatrice spreads her arms out and makes circles in the air, as if she is about to take off and fly.)

BEATRICE: Only after the bad thoughts. And the bitch. And the blood.

(Beatrice makes bigger circles with her arms. Faster and faster.)

BEATRICE: When all possible damage has been blooded and the floor is sticky and red with regret, only then does the sweet sweet bitch with the leaping, fire-fuelled thoughts finally open the doors and enter ... She's skin on skin, breath into the neck, just enough heat to warm but not cook. Just enough, to make you crave. A bit more. Just a little bit more. Please. Please, please, just a little bit more of the beautiful ... Belligerent. Bewildering ...

(Beatrice suddenly stops.)

BEATRICE: Beatrice.

(Beatrice leaps off the top of the wardrobe and lands on the bed, face first. She doesn't move for a long moment. Jamie enters the bedroom, dressed only in his jeans, holding two tumblers of dark, murky liquid.)

JAMIE: Let's party.

(Blackout.)

(Thumping techno music blasts from everywhere.)

SCENE THREE

(The Nightclub. The music continues to thump and pound. A moving neon light flicks and twists around the space and eventually lands on Jamie. With his coat buttoned up, he jumps up and down on the spot in the rhythm with the music. He is solely and completely in his own body, oblivious to everyone else in the Nightclub.)

SCENE FOUR

(The Bedroom. Night. Beatrice and Jamie sit at opposite ends of the bed, naked, wrapped up in the bedclothes. Silence, except for the hard breathing coming from both of them. Eventually ...)

BEATRICE: *(barely audible)* Bathroom?

JAMIE: Sorry?

BEATRICE: *(louder)* Can I use the bathroom?

JAMIE: Oh. Sure. Just through there.

BEATRICE: Thanks.

(Beatrice slowly gets up, stealing some of the bedclothes and wrapping herself up in it.)

JAMIE: It's dirty. Probably, you'll think it's dirty and I'm a complete pig. No. Not probably. Absolutely. I only just realised. I've never been on my own before. I'm disgusting. Sorry. I would have ... If I had known ... This ... If I had any idea that this ... I would have ...

(Beatrice stops beside Jamie.)

JAMIE: Cleaned.

(Beatrice tries to think of something to say. Instead, she lunges in and kisses him deeply. She pulls away and

heads to the door. Jamie watches her. Beatrice suddenly stops at the doorway and spins around, stares at Jamie, a horrified look on her face.)

JAMIE: What? … What?

(Beatrice runs out of the bedroom. The sound of a door slamming. Silence.)

JAMIE: Boom boom shaka shaka boom … Did you hear that music?

(Jamie leans out of the bed and grabs one of the glasses of dark, murky liquid. He sniffs it, pulls a face and puts it back.)

JAMIE: Boom boom shaka shaka boom … Do you go there a lot? I'm going to go there. A lot. It's good isn't it? … Yeah. Yeah, it's fine, excellent, pleasant, agreeable and gratifying … Boom boom shaka shaka boom … Yeah.

(Jamie leans over the side of the bed and grabs a bottle of water. He drinks it all. He throws the empty water bottle under the bed.)

JAMIE: You cheating on your bloke? … It's okay if you are. I'm not asking for anything …

(Jamie sits up and rifles through the clothing on the floor. He picks up the 'Kill All Babies' t-shirt and puts it on.)

JAMIE: I'm new around here. I'm all new … Needed to get out. See the world. Or at least a different part of it.

(Jamie flops back down on the bed.)

JAMIE: Family ... You can say anything you want ... I'm not a kid, I'm not a kid, look at me and see how much of a kid I'm not ... Nothing ever changes. It's all around and around and around ... You know what I mean?

(Jamie sits up, rips off the t-shirt and throws it on the floor and falls back onto the bed.)

JAMIE: I've got all these sisters. More than you can imagine or can be considered acceptable. They're everywhere, all of the time. Just this solid wall of hair and cackling that consistently proves to be a worthy advocate to normal human reasoning ... Bridget's alright. But the rest of them ... I'm not being mean. I'm really not ... Are you okay in there?

(Jamie sits up.)

JAMIE: … Hello?

(Beat. The bathroom door opens and slams shut. Jamie falls back onto the bed.)

JAMIE: It's the laugh on them. That's what belts at the heart … Belts at the heart. That's a good phrase isn't it?

(Jamie waits for an answer.)

JAMIE: *(to himself)* Good phrase … *(calling out)* Anyway, the laugh.

(Jamie lets out a high-pitched cackle.)

JAMIE: No. That's not it.

(Jamie tries another laugh.)

JAMIE: Not quite. Closer though … Anyway, that's all they do. Lock themselves in the bathroom and laugh the time away … Laugh the time away.

(Jamie digs under the bed and pulls out a notebook. Writes 'laugh the time away'. He puts the notebook back under the bed.)

JAMIE: You should see them. Hoarding themselves away, desperately trying to make the ugly less ugly. Go on, I say to them, standing like an idiot outside the door. Waiting. Always waiting. Go on and try ... Because they're the ugliest bunch you've ever seen. And that's not being mean either. That's just fact ... Slapping and scraping and slapping every last thing onto their faces. But still. Still ... Ugly will always be ugly ... You should see them.

(Beat. Jamie sits up on the bed.)

JAMIE: Wouldn't that be something? … If you saw them?

(Jamie jumps out of the bed and walks to the door.)

JAMIE: Sunday lunch.   All of them around the table. Jabbering on about everything and saying nothing. Words without meaning. Makes me so angry. Makes me ... But you. On my arm. Or just you. The moment would need nothing else but … That shocked, silent look on their faces. Because you would make them silent …You would open the bathroom door. You ...

(Jamie exits the bedroom.)

JAMIE: *(offstage)* Hey? Would you do that? Would you come with me? ... We could hide it from your bloke if you want ...

(Beat.   Jamie re-enters the bedroom, jumping up and down to music only he can hear.)

JAMIE: ... Boom boom shaka shaka boom. Boom boom shaka shak-

(Beatrice storms in from the bathroom, shaking, furious, her eyes red from crying.)

BEATRICE: Slut!

(Jamie stops. Silence. Beatrice storms up to Jamie, right up in his face.)

BEATRICE: Slut Slut Slut.

(Jamie tries to get away from Beatrice and hits the wall.)

JAMIE: What?

(Beatrice gets up in Jamie's face.)

BEATRICE: Slutslutslutslutslutsl-

JAMIE: *(in her face)* STOP!

(Silence. Beatrice steps away from Jamie.)

BEATRICE: Doesn't sound so good now, does it?

JAMIE: What?

(Beatrice lunges at Jamie.)

BEATRICE: Funny little boy. Funny funny little boy aren't we?

JAMIE: What? No. What?

(Jamie ducks away from Beatrice. She follows him as he moves around the room, trying to get away from her.)

BEATRICE: Big man with his big words. Because words are everything aren't they Jamie? Isn't that your thing? Words, words, it's all about the fucking words?

JAMIE: I don't understand.

BEATRICE: Slut.

(Jamie lunges at Beatrice.)

JAMIE: I DON'T UNDERSTAND!

(Beat. Beatrice pulls away from Jamie and walks to one side of the bed. Jamie remains in the same position.)

BEATRICE: I asked where the bathroom was.

JAMIE: … Okay.

(Beatrice calmly walks to the other end of the bed.)

BEATRICE: And then you were talking about being disgusting.

JAMIE: My sisters. I don't know how to use a bathroom because I have too many sisters. Because I only get these tiny tiny seconds and I have to do it all. It's all just madness. Time stops or beats to a different clock and there's no seconds left to put the towel away or scrape the hair from the sink. The seconds come and go and you have to grab as many as you can before your mother shouts that the bus is coming.

(Beat.)

BEATRICE: And then I made you hard just by sticking my tongue in your mouth.

JAMIE: … Yes.

BEATRICE: And then you said-

JAMIE: No.

(Beatrice walks to the doorway, faces away from Jamie.)

BEATRICE: Nice and low.

JAMIE: No.

(Silence. Beatrice suddenly turns around and storms up to Jamie. Jamie starts dancing on the spot as Beatrice approaches.)

JAMIE: No. No. No. No.

(Beatrice stops before she reaches Jamie.)

BEATRICE: What are you doing?

JAMIE: Boom boom shaka shaka boom-

BEATRICE: STOP!

(Jamie stops. Silence.)

BEATRICE: I should go.

(Beat. Beatrice suddenly moves, jerking around the bedroom, picking up every piece of clothing off the floor, including her own, and tossing them away. Jamie watches her.)

BEATRICE: Because I'm thirty-seven. Which isn't the problem. But thirty-seven and here? Oh yes, thirty-seven and here is ten problems. More, worse, and all of them scream of a messiness that should have been scraped away sometime before the clock struck thirty-seven. So I should go, and be thirty-seven someplace else.

(Beatrice stops.)

BEATRICE: Say something.

(Beat.)

JAMIE: I wouldn't say that.

(Beatrice continues moving around the room. Jamie watches her.)

BEATRICE: No.

JAMIE: It's not one of my words.

BEATRICE: Because cruel. Cruel. And mean ... And dark. And murky.

(Beatrice picks up her underwear and puts them on. Jamie starts dancing on the spot. Beat. Both of them stop and stare at each other. A long moment passes.)

BEATRICE: What? ... WHAT?

(Jamie drops to the floor and dives under the bed.)

BEATRICE: Because I was just trying to have some fun Jamie. Because there hasn't been a lot of fun lately to be found and why shouldn't I? At least close to it. You don't know. You will probably never know, because this is fast looking like it's about to come to a swift and slightly painful ending. And I know how painful the end is. But fun is exactly what the doctor ordered. Because nothing has happened. All of the effort you can possibly imagine, and not one thing has happened ... Perhaps I wanted too much. Too many things. Because I wanted to be everything. Absolutely everything. And you can't have that. And it's heartbreaking ... But none of that matters. Except I deserve, I really deserve, a little bit of fun. Just for one night. That doesn't make me a ... That doesn't make me anything but normal. Just normal. Because everyone wants everything. And everyone is lucky to end up with something ... But you know that ... Don't you? ... Because please. Please tell me you haven't been screwed up this young. Please tell me you are sweet and innocent and still slightly scared of women. Please say you haven't spent your teenage years wide-eyed and muscle sore thanks to free porn on the internet. Please tell me you're not moments away from slapping me on the arse and calling me worse than ...

(Jamie crawls out from under the bed, dragging a cardboard box. He shoves the box into Beatrice's arms.)

JAMIE: There. All of them are there ... See for yourself. See it.

(Beatrice holds the box but doesn't open them.)

JAMIE: Go on.

(Jamie rips the box open and pulls out fistfuls of note-books. He holds them up to Beatrice's face. Beat. Jamie throws the notebooks across the room. He pulls out an-other fistful of notebooks and holds them up to Beatrice's face. Jamie is about to throw them again-)

BEATRICE: I should go.

(Jamie drops all of the notebooks back into the box except one. He flicks through it, showing Beatrice the tight scrawl covering every inch of paper.)

JAMIE: Look. Look at them … Go on …

BEATRICE: Stop.

JAMIE: All of the words. Every last one of them. Go on. I don't care.

BEATRICE: Stop now.

(Beat. Jamie pushes Beatrice around the room, picking up the notebooks, shoving them into Beatrice's face, and then throwing them on the ground.)

JAMIE: Look. Read. Go on. Every last one of them. Because I don't care. Why would I care what you think? Who are you Beatrice? Who are you to be here in my place, my little little place, and tell me words that are not mine? Who are you?

(Jamie pushes Beatrice too hard. She trips and falls on the floor.)

JAMIE: Read them. Go on.

(Beatrice breathes hard, struggling for air.)

JAMIE: I dare you.

(Blackout.)

SCENE FIVE

(The Nightclub. The neon light bounces around with less intensity. Slow movements, as if the light is about to burn out. It stops on Jamie. He has lost his jacket and his t-shirt. He continues to jump with the thumping music. The music starts to slow. Jamie starts to slow with it. It continues until the music is a series of long, mechanical beeps.)

SCENE SIX

(The Hospital. Night. Beatrice lies unconscious in the hospital bed. The long, mechanical beeps continue rhythmically from unseen machines. Jamie sits on a plastic chair, his coat unbuttoned, his head between his legs, throwing up into a stainless steel bedpan. He finishes and slowly raises his head. He stares straight ahead, not once looking in Beatrice's direction.)

JAMIE: Then he asked me what happened. After he looked me up and down, taking his time about it, making me feel hot and stupid. After he asked me if I was your son and what our last name was ... After I didn't say anything because ...

(Jamie leans over, almost throws up, stops. Beat.)

JAMIE: Because what is happening? I don't understand what the fuck is happening.

(Jamie throws up again.)

JAMIE: Fuck ... That's not one of my words. No, that was never one of my words. Because my sisters used to say it all the time. Fuck him. And fuck her. And fuck everyone ... Not Bridget, but the rest ... I really want to call Bridget, but I can't call Bridget and say I don't understand what the fuck is happening. But I can't call Bridget. Because that is ... crazy ... He came in close, too close, a hand gripping my shoulder, pressing down on the flesh and the little bit of muscle. Gripping it all the way to the bone. Could feel the gun wedged hard against his hip as he said ...'Son'.

(Jamie takes deep breaths.)

JAMIE: 'Son, you need to tell me what happened' ... Little bit of cock in his voice. Only a little bit, and you could only hear it if you were listening for it. But it was absolutely there.

(Jamie leans forward. His body convulses, wanting to throw up again. Nothing comes out. He sits up.)

JAMIE: Why aren't you wearing a hat? Policeman have hats. You've got the gun and the badge and the little bit of cock in your voice, so where is your hat? Show me your fucking hat ... I'm liking that word more and more Beatrice ... Fucking Beatrice.

(Jamie lunges forward and coughs up some bile.)

JAMIE: This is not real. This is not happening. This can't be real. This can't be happening. This, this, this.

(Jamie lunges forward and tries to throw up. Painful. Violent. Nothing comes out.)

JAMIE: Because he doesn't have a hat. And policemen should have hats.

(Jamie puts the bedpan on the floor.)

JAMIE: With his hand still on my shoulder and his fin-
    gers.   Those fingers.   Full of muscles.   Fingers
    stronger than fingers should be.   Everything is all
    wrong with him, starting with the hat that is not there
    and ending with his big fingers bruising my bones ...
    'Son? ... Son!'

*(Beat. Jamie stands up, steps over the bedpan and walks
to the end of the bed.)*

JAMIE: I'M NOT HER FUCKING SON.   I DON'T
    KNOW WHO THE FUCK SHE IS. I DON'T FUCK-
    ING KNOW ANYTHING ... Said it like that too Bea-
    trice.   Said it loud and beautiful so it would look like I
    meant it.

*(Jamie sits back down, picks up the bedpan, puts it down
again, sticks his head between his legs.)*

JAMIE: Slut. Just a dirty dumb ... Wouldn't let me go
    and I thought Why not? Why the fuck not? Fucking,
    fuck, fucking, fuck, fuck, fuck ...

(Jamie stands up and buttons up his coat.)

JAMIE: This is not happening.   This is not real.   The
    words don't matter because you don't have a hat on
    your head and she fell on the floor and didn't get up
    again.

*(Jamie strides over to Beatrice and stares at her lifeless
body. After a moment, he tears off the blankets and grabs*

Beatrice's wrist. The mechanical beeps become quicker, louder, more furious. Jamie ignores them as he removes a gold bracelet from Beatrice's wrist.)

JAMIE: You know what I mean? Desperate. Just one of those with everything hanging out and slopping all over you. I should have walked away but I'm new around here and I'm taking it all. You know what I mean? Yeah. Yeah, you know what I mean. It was just there. Laid out over everything and giving it away for nothing. So I took it. I took it all. You know what I mean? Yeah … Yeah.

(Jamie covers Beatrice up again before calmly stepping over the bedpan and walking out the door. Beat. The room begins to fill with brilliant white light, coming from every direction and filling the space. Brighter, brighter until the bed and Beatrice are engulfed in it. The mechanical beeps become longer and longer until it is one continuous beep.)

SCENE SEVEN

(The Nightclub. The long mechanical beeps continue. The neon light smashes around the space, only catching darkness.)

SCENE EIGHT

(The Park Bench. Night.)

BEATRICE: *(from the bushes)* ... Hello?

(Beat. A rustling from a different part of the bushes.)

BEATRICE: *(from the bushes)* Oh. You're still here. That's ... Yeah. That's really ...

(The sound of Beatrice throwing up in the bushes.)

BEATRICE: *(from the bushes)* Look ... Here's the thing ... Look ... Because you seem nice. I don't know for sure, because I'm drunk. And I've only seen you in the dark. But you seem to be one of the nice ones. Mainly because you're still here ... Are you still here? ... Hello? ...

(Beat.)

JAMIE: *(from a different part of the bushes)* Hello.

BEATRICE: *(from the bushes)* Oh. That is nice. That really is very, very nice. And nice is good. Nice should be enough. Jesus, most days I'd give my kingdom for some simple nice. You know what I mean? ... If you could promise me nothing but some simple nice then I would ... Could you do that? ... Do you think you could just be nice and nothing else? ... Like forever?

(Silence.)

BEATRICE: *(from the bushes)* Don't answer that. I don't want ... Look. I'm just going to go home. Because now crazy has come to the party and ...

(Beatrice rustles in the bushes, coming closer and closer to the park bench.)

BEATRICE: Look ... Look ... I'm just going to say some things and maybe you'll understand but maybe you won't, and I'm not quite sure it matters either way. And probably I should say nothing. Just go and you can just think I'm a bitch for a while and then not think about me at all.

(Beatrice stops moving in the bushes. Beat.)

BEATRICE: I'm thirty-seven years old. How did that happen? Because a moment ago, it was all endless. And now the doors are shutting. They are. I can hear the bang, bang, bang of the wood as the wind picks up and blows through. Thirty-seven, thirty-seven ... And nothing to call my own. I am thirty-seven years old and fucked too much and loved too little and time after time, failed to see that the difference is tinier than they should be ... Don't try and make sense of this. Don't you dare.

(Beat.)

BEATRICE: Are you making sense of this?

(Beat.)

BEATRICE: Are you still there?

(Beatrice comes out of the bushes dragging her large handbag. Her hair is out and wild with leaves and twigs stuck through it. She stops at the park bench and looks around.)

BEATRICE: Hello?

(Beat. Beatrice sits down on the park bench.)

SCENE NINE

(The Bedroom. Day. Jamie is tangled up in the sheets, crying and trying not to cry. The crying becomes fiercer, nudging at hysteria. Jamie lets out a long, piercing roar. The crying slowly starts to subside. Beat. Jamie disentangles himself from the sheets. He stands up, finds the 'Kill All Babies' t-shirt and puts it on. He lies back down in the bed and tries to sleep. Beat. He stands up, rips the shirt off and throws it on the floor. He picks up his coat and digs in the pocket. He pulls out the gold bracelet and puts it on his wrist. He gets back into bed, closes his eyes. Lights start to fade.)

JAMIE: Boom boom shaka shaka boom ... Boom boom ... boom.

SCENE TEN

(The Nightclub. The music thumps and pounds. The neon light shines on one spot on a wall. After a moment, the sound of a glass falling to the floor and smashing. Beat. The sound of a woman, perhaps Beatrice, screaming. A moment later, Jamie slams up against the wall, the light shining on him. He breathes hard. He rips open his jacket and tries to catch his breath.)

SCENE ELEVEN

(The Bedroom. Night. Jamie stands at the doorway holding both glasses of murky liquid. Beatrice lies on the bed, curled up into the foetal position, a wet towel covering her face.)

JAMIE: Okay ... Okay.

(Beat. Jamie strides around the room, spilling liquid from the glasses.)

JAMIE: I'm just going to ... I'm going to ... Beatrice? ... I'm going to have to ...

(Jamie stops at the end of the bed, stares at Beatrice. He leans in slowly and gently touches Beatrice's foot with one of the glasses. Beatrice pulls away, groans like an animal being tortured. Jamie jumps back, continues striding around the room. He gulps from one of the glasses.)

JAMIE: Because I really shouldn't be here. I don't know what's happening and I don't think it should be happening because I'm not really supposed to be here.

(Jamie stops, facing away from Beatrice.)

JAMIE: I'm adopted. I just found out. Because of Bridget. But not because of Bridget ... That's why I'm here ... No. Wait.

(Jamie downs the rest of one of the glasses. It goes down hard.)

JAMIE: I found out I was adopted and suddenly home was not home.

(Jamie throws the glass on the floor.)

JAMIE: So now I'm here. And this is happening. And I'm just going to ... Not understand it. I'm going to make that choice.

(Jamie drinks the second glass of dark murky liquid. Slow, savouring it. It still goes down hard. He stares at the empty glass for a moment and then clutches it hard between his hands. Beat. He laughs. He stops. He laughs again. The glass breaks in his hands. The shards fall to the floor. Jamie stares at his untouched, uncut hands. Beat. Jamie strides around the room.)

JAMIE: Okay ... That was the first thought ... Okay. And? ... Because it's just blood. Right? And blood is just blood ...

(Jamie stops, drops to his knees, caresses Beatrice's foot. Beatrice groans and moves away. Jamie continues to caress it. Beatrice eventually gives into it.)

JAMIE: When she got hit. When she was just coming home after her shift at the hospital ... When he didn't kill her but almost ... When they took her back to the hospital and said if we can get her blood, maybe if we can get her blood ... When I ripped off my shirt and said Me. All of it. Me ... That's when I found out. That's when I fell off the beat and couldn't find the space to fall into.

43

(Jamie laughs, a high-pitched cackle.)

JAMIE: That's it. That's the way they laugh. Those sisters that are not my sisters. One starts, tries to stop, then another starts and then it is everything. Everywhere.

(Jamie rubs Beatrice's foot. Harder and harder until Beatrice's starts to groan in pain again.)

JAMIE: Shouldn't have been laughing ... Not with me. Not with Bridget. Bridget wouldn't know how to laugh like that. She was ...

(Jamie suddenly stops, stands up, and strides around the room.)

JAMIE: I don't want to think about what she was. Because for a moment I thought okay. Okay. So it's one of those stories. Not my sister, but my mother. Okay, okay. Everything is okay. My blood is her blood. Okay, okay. I don't want to think about this Beatrice. When my blood was her blood and it was just me and her and perhaps amongst the blood everything could be perfect. When my Mum who isn't my Mum said 'Son. No. No, this is what happened.' When I slapped her so hard she fell into a wall. When I was angry. When I was just so angry ... When she said 'I wanted a boy so much I went and got one' and my hand was to her face quicker than words could ever come. When the sisters who aren't the sisters started to scream and attack. When I just looked at it all and felt myself having to become new.

(Jamie stops.)

JAMIE: But if I don't think about that, about the blood and not being able to spill it, about Bridget and not being able to help her, I will have to think about this. And I can't. I really, really ...

(Jamie rushes up to Beatrice.)

JAMIE: We should go to the hospital ... Should we go to the hospital?   I've got blood and maybe you can have it ... Beatrice?

(Beat. Jamie pulls away from Beatrice.)

JAMIE: I don't know where the hospital is.   I just grabbed things and said things and caught a train and then got off when a man with a hat said 'This is the end'.

(Jamie lunges into Beatrice.)

JAMIE: Liar. Fucking liars. Fucking, fucking- ... The words came so easily but got stuck in my mouth. Stuck and festering and giving me bad breath.

(Jamie pulls back, picks up his jeans and puts them on. He walks to the doorway and stops.)

JAMIE: I should call my Mum. Because my Mum knows all these things ...

(Jamie exits the room. Beatrice continues to lie on the bed. Beat. Jamie re-enters, holding the half-empty bottle of murky liquid. Jamie drinks steadily from it as he stands at the foot of the bed, staring at Beatrice.)

JAMIE: My sister lost the sight in one eye from a carrot peeler. We still don't know how that happened. And then another sister, this is Mary-Rose, she broke her thumb four times in one year ... That was the same year Teresa almost burnt her skin off with some cheap fake tan she bought on holiday in Thailand. And the others too. And it was all fine. It all turned out fine ... Except Bridget.

(Jamie leans in to Beatrice.)

JAMIE: I don't understand. Hospitals and emergencies and what we're supposed to do now. Sorry. Sorry. Because I've got all this knowledge. You know. You've seen all my words. But knowledge is funny isn't it? Both ha-ha and weird. All this knowledge, but none of it can help us right now ... Can they? ... All this knowledge and it's just making me weak and watery and completely useless ... Beatrice? Beatrice, I need you to say something. Can you ... Or sit up. Or make this stop. Talk to me about your Dad again. Or, or, suck my cock. Or dance. Just move your hips again. Just once. Because that's what this should be. This night. Dancing and sucking and telling each other stories. Don't you think?

46

(Jamie finishes the bottle of alcohol and drops it on the floor. He steps closer to Beatrice.)

JAMIE: Beatrice? ... Don't you think? ... Beatrice? ... I need you to ... Beatrice ... I want my Mum Beatrice.

(Beat. Jamie crawls onto the bed and curls up next to Beatrice. They lie together for a long moment. Slowly, carefully, Beatrice removes the towel from her face. She's been crying. She takes long, deep breaths as she slowly sits up in the bed. Jamie moves closer to her and rests his head in her lap. Beat. Beatrice strokes his hair.)

JAMIE: Softer.

(Beatrice strokes his hair softer.)

JAMIE: Now tell me something.

(Beatrice continues to stroke Jamie's hair.)

JAMIE: Tell me ... Tell me everything is as solid as I want it to be. That even though the world looks like a thin sheet of glass, don't worry. Don't give it another thought. Because I can trust you. You will hold the world up, no matter how many times I thump and pound and try to break it.

(Beat.)

BEATRICE: No.

(Beat.)

JAMIE: Softer.

(Beatrice softly strokes his hair.)

JAMIE: … Almost.

(Beatrice leans into Jamie and repeatedly kisses his head.)

JAMIE: Yes ...Yes.

(Beatrice continues kissing Jamie's head, the emotion coming slowly. She carefully slides down into the bed and continues kissing Jamie all over his head and face. The lights slowly start to fade. Beatrice pulls Jamie closer and closer. Jamie curls into Beatrice and falls asleep. Beatrice closes her eyes. Blackout.)

BEATRICE: *(repeated)* Boom boom shaka shaka boom. Boom boom shaka shaka boom.

(Silence. Lights up. Jamie lies in the bed. Beatrice stands at the end of the bed, dressed in her underwear and Jamie's 'Kill The Babies' T-shirt. She holds a bunch of clothes in each hand and is doing an intense, complicated cheerleading dance.)

BEATRICE: BOOM BOOM SHAKA SHAKA BOOM. Goooooo WILDCATS!

(Beatrice jumps up and down, cheering wildly. Jamie watches on without emotion. Beatrice stops and leans on the edge of the bed, her head down, breathing hard. Beat.)

BEATRICE: No. No, I'm okay. It's not ... I used to be able to do that ten times in a row, drink a bottle of tequila and still want something more. But that was a long time ago. God, that was a long, long time ago ... Don't worry. It's not ... That was something else. It's nothing serious. Although you shouldn't have ... Doesn't matter. I was probably being a bitch. I'm losing drinks. Don't worry about it. I'm glad I'm still here. Happy ... A virus. Just one of those viruses with some long, complicated name that make it sound like death. But it's not death. Not for me ... It's just a moment. It's always just a moment ... Sorry. Sorry Jamie. That wasn't supposed to happen. None of this was supposed to happen. I was just looking for fun ... Just some crazy fun. It's crazy, right? It's just crazy ... Can I get some water? ... Please?

(Beatrice looks up.)

BEATRICE: ... What?

(Jamie quickly leans over and pulls out another bottle of water, half-empty. He holds it out to Beatrice. Beat.)

BEATRICE: WHAT!

(Beat.)

BEATRICE: Oh, you think ...

JAMIE: It's water.

BEATRICE: What do you think?

JAMIE: Have some water.

BEATRICE: That I'm one of those girls? That I'm just a girl? Just another one of those girls?

JAMIE: You asked for water. Here I am, giving you water.

(Beat. Beatrice knocks the bottle of water out of Jamie's hand.)

BEATRICE: Fuck your water. And fuck you. Who the hell ... I mean, who the hell? ... What are you? Twelve years old? Are you twelve years old Jamie?

JAMIE: No.

BEATRICE: It was just a thing Jamie. Just one of those things that start to happen to remind you that time is passing and will eventually run out. One of those things Jamie ... Jamie ... Jamie ... How perfect is Jamie? ... Little boy name for the little boy. Who gets angry and throws little tantrums. Who sulks in his bed when he doesn't get to fuck and suck and take what he wants. Isn't that right Jamie? Jamie. Jamie. It's all about little bloody fucking little Jamie.

(Beat.)

JAMIE: You should go.

BEATRICE: I'm not going.

JAMIE: You really should go.

BEATRICE: I'm not going.

JAMIE: You scared me.

(Beatrice stops.)

JAMIE: You were on the floor ...

(Beatrice comes closer.)

JAMIE: Don't ... Don't get all ... You didn't move.

BEATRICE: It doesn't matter.

JAMIE: It doesn't matter?

BEATRICE: Just a moment.

JAMIE: You started to go cold.

(Beat.)

JAMIE: No. Right. What does it matter? ... Because it's all just some fun isn't it Beatrice? It's all just ... Amusement, festivity, conviviality-

(Beatrice rushes up to Jamie, almost kisses him.)

BEATRICE: ... You want to fight with me?

JAMIE: ... You scared me.

BEATRICE: I'm sorry.

JAMIE: I can't be new and scared. I don't think I can do that. I think I will break. Just fall and break. You know what I mean?

BEATRICE: ... No.

JAMIE: Just-

BEATRICE: You won't break. It will come close. It will feel like it, but it won't happen.

(Jamie dances on the spot.)

JAMIE: It feels like it. It feels like it might happen right now.

(Beatrice grabs at Jamie, tries to make him stop. Jamie pushes her away and dances harder, working himself into a frenzy. Beatrice watches him, helpless. Jamie eventually stops. He breathes hard. He falls onto the bed. Beat.)

JAMIE: Boom boom shaka shaka boom.

(Beat.)

JAMIE: Boom boom shaka shaka-

BEATRICE: Jamie-

(Jamie stands up suddenly.)

JAMIE: Did you hear it? ... That music. Did you hear it?

BEATRICE: No.

JAMIE: I want that music. I want it all the time. In my head and in my body and just always.

(Jamie begins to dance. Slow, exaggerated movements.)

JAMIE: Walking down these streets. Being all new and angry and just walking around. Reading the names of the streets and the words have no meaning. You're just flesh. Just all flesh and all muscle, surrounded by words that have no meaning. New. Unknown. Untried, untouched and untrodden.

(Beat. Beatrice starts to mimic Jamie's moves. Jamie moves around the room. Beatrice follows behind.)

JAMIE: Cooper and Watergreen. Keep walking. Sunshine Avenue and Bluebell Boulevard. Keep walking. Steven Street and Caitlin Lane. Windsor and Birdie and back to Cooper. Watergreen. Sunshine. Bluebell. Bluebell. Bluebell. Stop.

(Jamie stops. Beatrice stops.)

JAMIE: Can you hear it?

BEATRICE: No.

(Jamie squats down.)

JAMIE: Down low. Deep. Beneath the surface.

(Beatrice squats down. Jamie starts to bounce up and down on the balls of his feet.)

JAMIE: All new. All angry. And just walking around. You need a word but it's all Sunshine and Bluebell. You want to scream because Bridget didn't scream and now you can't call her and ask her what that word might be.

(Beat. Jamie continues bouncing up and down. Beatrice watches him.)

BEATRICE: Jamie?

(Jamie jumps up, dances around the room. Beatrice doesn't move.)

JAMIE: Bluebell, bluebell, bluebell. You start to hear it on Bluebell. That music. Not quite music. That music. Bluebell, bluebell, bluebell. Right at the end and down. Down, down, down and that music that is not quite music.

(Jamie stops and dances on the spot.)

JAMIE: Down, down, down, shaka, shaka ... down. Boom, boom, shaka, shaka ... boom ... Did you hear it? Boom boom shaka shaka ... boom.

(Jamie stops dancing.)

JAMIE: It's the spaces. If you listen hard enough, you can find the spaces in the music. And it's all you want. It's what you need, but it's also all you want. New and angry and all new, you're just looking for a space to drop and fall into. To stop being so new. To maybe stop being so angry. I love that music. I've been trying to keep on top of the beat and all the time I just had to find the space to fall into ... Because look. Look what happens. You.

(Beat. Beatrice starts to bounces up and down on the balls of her feet. Jamie watches her.)

BEATRICE: Boom, boom, shaka, shaka ... boom.

(Beatrice slowly rises, dancing on the spot.)

BEATRICE: Boom, boom, shaka, shaka ... boom. Boom boom shaka shaka ...

(Beatrice stops. Silence. Jamie grabs Beatrice and kisses her.)

SCENE TWELVE

(The Hospital. Beatrice lies in the bed with the wires and tubes coming in and out of her. Long, mechanical beeps pulse rhythmically. Beatrice shakes violently. The beeps become louder, faster, manic. Beatrice's hand shoots out, the gold bracelet on her wrist. She grabs at the air. Beat. Beatrice drops her hand. The shaking slowly calms down until Beatrice is still and silent. The mechanical beeps return to a long, steady pulse. Beat. The door flies open and Jamie storms in. He stops, stares at Beatrice. He is sweating, sick. He rips his coat off and throws it on the chair. He paces around.)

JAMIE: You need to ... What you need to do is ... Because this moment, this little moment of yours, where you scare the hell out of us and then you're suddenly fine ... You need to move to the fine bit now ... Open your eyes. Open them now. Eyes on eyes Beatrice. That's what needs to happen. Now. Now. Show me your eyes Beatrice. Now, now ... NOW!

(Beat. Jamie grabs the bedpan and sits down on the chair. He leans forward, about to throw up.)

SCENE THIRTEEN

(The Nightclub. Thumping, pounding music. The neon light shines on Jamie standing against the wall. Beat. Beatrice comes rushing up to him, the front of her dress wet. She gets up in his face, berating him for spilling a drink on her. The words are furious and loud but the music is louder. Jamie tries to apologise and when that doesn't work, he tries to get away from her. Beatrice belts him with her handbag. Jamie grabs her by the shoulders, spins her around and slams her against the wall. They stare at each other. Eye to eye. A moment of sudden, full-throttled lust. Beatrice lunges into Jamie, tries to kiss him. Jamie pulls back. Beatrice is offended. Jamie indicates for her to wait. Beatrice stands impatiently against the wall, the neon light shining in her furious face. She stomps away. A moment later, she walks across the light. A moment later, she walks back, crosses her arms, yells obscenities, waits. The music thumps and pounds. Beat. Jamie enters the light. He thrusts a brightly coloured alcoholic drink into her face. Beatrice hesitates for a moment before taking the drink and gulping from it.)

SCENE FOURTEEN

(The Park Bench. Day. Jamie sits on the park bench, wrapped up in his coat. He plays with the gold bracelet.)

JAMIE: No ... No ... One more ... Helium? No. But good try. Helium is a good word. Scientists are good with words aren't they? I thought about science for a while. Giving the years to that. But no ... No. I don't think that will happen now. I don't think much will happen even though I really would like it to ... Maybe the words will do something. Come together in the right order. Maybe ... Try another one. No. One more. Just one more ... Hello? ... Hello. Nice. It could have been that. Maybe it should have been that simple. But it wasn't simple, was it? ...

(Jamie fights back tears.)

JAMIE: I'm not going to remember that. I don't think that's a good idea. Not the Hellos and not the Good-byes but maybe just the middle. Just the bits in between ... Or, perhaps none of it. I won't tell anyone ... I'll want to. There will be moments where I will want to play it like a winning card. But I won't. Or, at least, try ... One more. Just one more ... Hyperbole? Goddamn. How good is that? No. Keep going. Give me another one. Please ... I'm young. I'm younger than I think, so I don't know how good I'm going to be. I'll probably tell this story to get a girl to like me. Or just to fuck me. I'll probably do that because I'm young. I'm younger than I think ... Go on. One more ...

(Jamie takes deep breaths.)

JAMIE: Because beginnings and endings are hard. Confusing, and full of lies. The ridiculous promises. The chest beating and ruffles of flesh thrust out on display. None of that. Just the middle. Just the parts where the mind unclenches and the words have a clear path ... One more ... Hubris? Hubris. Fuck me, you're good at this. You are so good at this. Your Dad taught you well. He'd be proud of you. Can I say that? Can I say everything now? ... One more ... Just one more ... Come on. Please. Just one more please. Please. Please ... Please.

(Jamie stands up.)

JAMIE: Okay. Okay, you win. You win Beatrice ... Home. H is for home. Home. Because of the shape. The shape you have to make with your mouth. Home. Can you see? It's a hole. You have to make a hole to make a home. Not many people think about that ... Don't you think?

(Beat. Jamie slowly feeds the bracelet into his mouth and swallows it. Jamie sits down on the park bench. He pulls out the butt of a joint from his coat pocket and lights it. He sits smoking the joint. Blackout.)

SCENE FIFTEEN

(The Park Bench. Night. Beatrice sits clutching her large handbag to her chest.)

BEATRICE: You could have said ... Something. Like, goodbye. Goodbye is a good word. No hard feelings, but ... Something. Anything. Because you're old enough to know better. You can't claim young on being a dick ... Goodbye Beatrice. Can't do this so gotta go. Not that hard ... is it? ... Pussy ... Nothing but a PUSSY!

(Beatrice unpacks her enormous handbag, searching for something. She pulls out a change of clothes, a bulging toiletries bag, a book, various papers and unopened envelopes.)

BEATRICE: I don't need this ... I mean, I'll be fine. You're just a person. Just a jumping, thumping, spilling drinks on women, person. With your shit about music and spaces and ... But I'll be fine. It will all go on. And on. Good and bad and in the end, it evens out as fine ... My walls were talking to me. That's the only reason I'm here, but it'll all even out.

(Beat. Beatrice finds a rumpled joint at the bottom of her bag. She smooths it out and searches through the bag for a lighter.)

BEATRICE: I covered the red wall with pictures and paintings. Nice things. Calming. But red can't be stopped. Refuses to be tamed.

(Beatrice finds a lighter and tries to light the joint but can't get it to work. Beatrice throws the lighter into the bushes.)

BEATRICE: Because I'm trying to have a different kind of life. I've been running in circles, the same ones, but I didn't know that when I was running ... I need to sit down more. Take deep breaths. I need to let the thoughts, all of them, come out and walk about and take a nap and find their own place in the world. Or something. Because I'm tired. I'm so fucking tired and there's still so much more to go.

(Beatrice starts to repack her bag with one hand while holding the joint with the other.)

BEATRICE: So I'm trying. I'm sitting in a chair with a book and a glass of wine, telling myself, this is a night. This can be a night ... It's a good book. About an affair that starts on a plane and then the plane crashes. And trauma turns to love. Which seems a good a path as any ... Right? ... Hello? ... Sneaky, sneaky, coward, flooding into the night ... I'm not telling you what the wall said. You're not getting my crazy. Even though you're not here ... You're not here are you? ... Hello?

(Beat.)

BEATRICE: I was out of there so fast. That familiar fury banging and slapping against my brain. Get out, get out. Run and don't come back. Run and run all the way to ... I shouldn't have gone there. Because I need to sit. I need to ...

(Beatrice zips up in the handbag and holds it to her chest. Beatrice sticks the joint in her mouth. Waits. Silence. Jamie comes out of the bushes, holding the bottle of dark, murky liquid.)

JAMIE: Look what I found. Look.

(Beatrice doesn't move.)

JAMIE: I heard this noise and I thought it was you ... Are you alright?

(Beatrice nods.)

JAMIE: Okay. Well, I didn't know that. Because I went looking. In the bushes. There's things in there. A whole world ... Look. Alcohol. Free. For us.

(Jamie digs into his coat pocket and pulls out the gold bracelet.)

JAMIE: And look. I found this too ... Would you like it? ...

(Jamie holds it out to Beatrice. Beatrice doesn't move.)

JAMIE: It's nice ... Don't you think? And it's not steal-ing. I didn't take it. I found it. That's the differ-ence ... Would you like it?

(Beat. Beatrice nods. Jamie puts the bracelet on Bea-trice's wrist.)

JAMIE: There. There, look at that. Like it was meant to be ... Don't you think?

(Beat. Jamie digs into his other pocket and pulls out a lighter. He flicks the flame and holds it out to Beatrice. Beatrice stares at the flame for a long moment before leaning forward and lighting the joint. Blackout. The glow of the joint as it is passes back and forth between Jamie and Beatrice.)

SCENE SIXTEEN

(The Hospital. Day. Thumping, pounding nightclub music. The empty bed is now stripped bare. The wires and machines have been removed. The bedpan has been cleaned and sits on the bedside table.)

SCENE SEVENTEEN

(The Bedroom. Night. Beatrice sits at one end of the bed, wrapped up in the bedclothes. Jamie is curled up at the other end, also wrapped up in bedclothes. Jamie's notebooks are thrown about the room. Beatrice hands the lit joint to Jamie.)

BEATRICE: Come on.

(Jamie takes the joint and smokes it.)

JAMIE: No.

(Jamie hands the joint back to Beatrice. She shakes her head.)

BEATRICE: Come on.

(Jamie puts the joint out on the side of the wardrobe.)

JAMIE: I don't know what you want.

BEATRICE: One.

JAMIE: I don't understand.

(Jamie holds the burnt out joint towards Beatrice.)

BEATRICE: No. You keep it ... Just one.

(Beat.)

JAMIE: Tree.

BEATRICE: No ... One more.

(Jamie looks for a place to put the joint.)

JAMIE: I can't ... I have nothing ... Absolutely nothing.

BEATRICE: I don't believe you.

(Jamie finds his coat and sticks the joint in the pocket.)

JAMIE: It can't work like that. You can't just keep asking. I don't understand ... Tibet.

BEATRICE: No. But nice.

JAMIE: Table.

BEATRICE: No.

JAMIE: Timber.

BEATRICE: No.

JAMIE: Territory.

BEATRICE: No.

JAMIE: … Testicle?

BEATRICE: Definitely no.

JAMIE: Then I quit.

BEATRICE: One more. I can't believe you've never played this. You and your words ...

JAMIE: … Tea.

BEATRICE: I love this game. No.

JAMIE: Teacup.

BEATRICE: I haven't played it in years. Years and years.

JAMIE: Teacups? Is that it?

BEATRICE: It's crazy. Crazy I even thought of it ... Teacups?

JAMIE: Yes.

BEATRICE: No.

JAMIE: Then I give up. Really. That was the last one.

BEATRICE: One more.

(Jamie grabs more of the bedclothes and wraps himself in it. Beatrice lets him take it.)

JAMIE: This is not the way it works. This is ... Words shouldn't be forced. Not ... plucked. Not ripped from the soil like a dirty, useless weed   Not ... Tarantula.

BEATRICE: Tarantula. Good one. No.

JAMIE: ... I'm starting to get angry now. I don't want to be angry. But I'm starting to feel it.

(Beatrice slowly crawls towards Jamie.)

BEATRICE: Don't.

JAMIE: I am.

BEATRICE: There's nothing to be angry about. It's good. It's really good. Come on.

JAMIE: I've got no more.

BEATRICE: You've got plenty more ... All those words. Look at them.

(Beatrice climbs on top of Jamie and kisses him all over.)

JAMIE: No. No more. You've got them all. Taken them. Just taken them.

BEATRICE: No.

JAMIE: Yes.

BEATRICE: Keep going. I didn't take them. I wouldn't do that. Keep going. Please.

JAMIE: But I don't understand it.

(Beatrice stops kissing Jamie.)

BEATRICE: It's easy. Guess the word and then you get that as a present. Yours starts with a 'T'.

(Beatrice kisses Jamie on the mouth.)

JAMIE: That's simple.

BEATRICE: Right.

JAMIE: Not easy. Simple.

BEATRICE: What?

JAMIE: … I don't like presents.

(Beatrice climbs off Jamie and lies across the bed. Jamie covers her with the bedclothes.)

BEATRICE: That's not true.

JAMIE: I hate them.

BEATRICE: No. No one thinks that. Presents are great.

JAMIE: Presents think they are great.

BEATRICE: What does that mean?

(Under the bedclothes, Jamie's hand moves up Beatrice's leg.)

JAMIE: I don't know ... Tasmania?

BEATRICE: ... No.

(Jamie runs his hand up and down Beatrice's thigh, slowly climbing higher and higher. Beatrice responds to his touch.)

JAMIE: Presents are empty.   Just ...

BEATRICE: Empty?

JAMIE: The wrapping and then the ribbon and making it all look ... Terrific?

(Beatrice shakes her head.)

JAMIE: But it's not terrific. It's never terrific. It's just ... socks. And not even good socks.

BEATRICE: What are good socks?

(Jamie begins to masturbate Beatrice under the covers.)

JAMIE: I don't know, but you'll never find them wrapped up in thick paper and shiny ribbon. That's never what you find. Never ... Normal socks. And normal being boring. Normal meaning average. Not your best work and not your worst. Average socks. That's all you're getting in your fussily wrapped package. Nothing but average socks ...

(Jamie stops.)

JAMIE: Tippy-toes?

(Beatrice sits up.)

BEATRICE: Tippy-toes?

(Jamie pulls Beatrice closer to him and continues to masturbate her.)

JAMIE: Or worse. People think they know you. Which is worse than average. Which is ... Terrible?

BEATRICE: No ... No.

JAMIE: The wrapping comes off and it's just yet another piece of normal but that's to be expected. That's not the terrible part. It's the look on their faces. Pride shooting out of every pore. No words, but the sentence is plain. I nailed this.

BEATRICE: More.

JAMIE: No. No, you didn't. There was no nailing of anything. Not even close. The anger Beatrice. All this red, red anger ... And who the hell do you think you are? I mean, really? You don't know me. Why are you even buying me a present? Why are you doing that? And that's all it is. That's all that presents become. Resentment and anger and evidence that no one will ever know you as well as you need them to.

(Beatrice orgasms. Silence.)

BEATRICE: What is tippy-toes?

(Beat. Jamie leaps up from the bed and walks up and down on his toes.)

JAMIE: Tippy-toes. See? Tippy-toes.

BEATRICE: ... No.

(Jamie stops, stares at his feet. Beat.)

BEATRICE: It's a good present.

JAMIE: How do I know that?

BEATRICE: ... Because it's always a good present. That's the game.

JAMIE: ... Teapots.

BEATRICE: No.

(Jamie grabs the bedclothes and pulls them off the bed, exposing Beatrice's naked body. He wraps himself up in them and stands in the corner. Beatrice doesn't move from the bed.)

BEATRICE: You'll like it.

JAMIE: No. I'm done now. I'm done with all of this. I didn't even want to play in the first place. This is not what I want to do with words. This is not anything I want to do.

(Beat. Beatrice rolls over and sits on the edge of the bed. She searches on the floor for her clothes.)

BEATRICE: You're just like me. I played the game like this. Done and did before the game had really even begun. But I was a child back then.

(Beatrice stops.)

BEATRICE: That's the last time I played this. With my Dad. He always had the best presents.

JAMIE: Like what?

(Beatrice continues to search for her clothes.)

BEATRICE: Doesn't matter.

JAMIE: Tell me.

BEATRICE: No. They don't matter later. Only in the moment ... He never gave in though. Never. I would plead and cry and get furious but still. Never.

JAMIE: Tickle.

BEATRICE: No ... But close ...

(Jamie crawls onto the bed and watches Beatrice.)

BEATRICE: Moving and thrashing and throwing my tiny body around. One more I thought. One more tantrum and I'll have him.

JAMIE: Tantrum.

BEATRICE: No. He was always stronger. Always had just a little bit more than me. But on that last morning, I was sick of it. Done.

JAMIE: Teacakes.

(Beatrice stops.)

BEATRICE: Teacakes?

JAMIE: Little cakes ... That you have with tea ... They're good. You think they're going to be just cake. But they're not. They're more than cake.

(Beatrice turns away, finds her dress and puts it on.)

BEATRICE: Threw my weight. Everything I had. Tested the muscles and bones. Learned what I could do ...

(Beatrice stands up, goes to the corner and finds her boots. She leans against the wall and puts them on. Jamie curls up in the bed.)

BEATRICE: Not much it turns out. Not enough. More drama than substance, which is probably a neat and accurate summary of my life so far ... That little body. I've dreamt it. That little useless body. Dreamt it hard. Trying, desperate, to twist and turn and change the dream. Desperate to make the body bigger. Stronger.

(Beatrice lunges towards Jamie and touches him.)

BEATRICE: Like yours.

(Beat.)

JAMIE: Talisman, Timbuktu, Toggle, Tar, Ten times Ten.

(Beatrice pulls away.)

BEATRICE: I tried. Tried hard. Turned away from him. Terrible, terrific screaming coming from me.

JAMIE: Turbulence.

BEATRICE: Yes.

(Jamie sits up.)

JAMIE: Yes?

BEATRICE: No, but yes. Our first turbulence. I'm somewhere else now. I'm sorry. You must think I'm crazy.

JAMIE: No.

(Beatrice slaps her hands on her face.)

BEATRICE: I shouldn't be doing this. *(to herself)* Stop doing this.

(Beatrice feels her ears, realises that her earrings are missing. She drops to the floor and searches for them.)

BEATRICE: Head in the pillow. Still screaming. And my Dad just standing there. Wrapped up in his uniform and feeling proud to have a job and a uniform. He would never say that. Not that kind of man. Silent. Strong. And none of those things getting in the way of love. One of those men. You know what I mean?

(Beatrice stops searching and sits on the floor.)

JAMIE: Yes.

BEATRICE: ... One more.

JAMIE: No.

BEATRICE: You have one more.

JAMIE: No. You keep talking.

BEATRICE: One more.

JAMIE: Truck.

BEATRICE: He stayed strong. Stayed that way for a long time. Longer than he should have. Longer than I deserved. But he had to turn. The minutes ticked away and eventually he had to turn and leave ... One more.

JAMIE: No.

BEATRICE: One more and then I'll ...

JAMIE: What?

BEATRICE: ... He was a bus driver. Which used to be a good job before the free world decided we all had to go to University and have careers. A good job that he liked and was proud of. Can you ask for more than that?

JAMIE: No ... Tears?

BEATRICE: That morning a woman got on. Normal. Average. Until he closed the doors behind her and was about to pull away. Then things stopped being normal. Or average.

JAMIE: Taliban? No.

BEATRICE: Because there was a fist on the glass. Bang, bang, bang. He was a proud man. But he was also a simple man. A simple, kind man who did simple, kind things. Bang, bang, bang.

JAMIE: Tickety-boo.

BEATRICE: He had a body. The man with the fist. Big and strong and capable of every thought his mind could conjure up. Big thoughts. Big and black and all of them focused on the woman. My dad tried to match him. Stood in front of the woman and willed his simple, kind thoughts to be enough. But it wasn't. Of course it wasn't. Because the world is crazy and crazy kills good people for no reason ... T is for tongue. I was going to suck your cock.

(Silence. Beatrice grabs her handbag.)

JAMIE: Stay ... Not to ... Or you can, but ... You can just stay ... For the night or ... Until you can face your red wall.

(Beat. Beatrice drops her handbag. Beatrice's breathing changes. She kneads the skin over her heart.)

77

JAMIE: What?

BEATRICE: Sorry.

(Jamie sits up.)

JAMIE: What? What's happening?

BEATRICE: Sorry ... I just ... I just need to pee. I'm losing drinks. Sorry.

(Beatrice rushes into the bathroom. Jamie moves around in the bed, trying to out different suggestive poses. He gets more and more entangled in the bed sheets until he is close to being suffocated.)

JAMIE: You're right. It is a good game. I mean, it's a sad story, a really sad story ... I'll talk like that one day. About Bridget ... You're smart Beatrice. Really smart. I've never met anyone like you. I mean, I've had girls. But you're not a girl. Because girls play different games. And not one of them ends with someone sucking your cock. What other games do you have? Because I'll play them all. Every last-

(A loud crash comes from the bathroom. Jamie stops.)

JAMIE: ... Hello?

SCENE EIGHTEEN

(The Nightclub. The thumping music. The neon light flashes around the space, catching nothing but darkness. The music becomes faster, louder, and then suddenly stops. The light stops, illuminating a door in the corner. On the other side of the room, Jamie can be heard jumping up and down.)

BEATRICE: ... Hello?

(Jamie stops jumping.)

JAMIE: Hello.

BEATRICE: What happened?

JAMIE: I don't know ... It just stopped. Bam.

BEATRICE: Bam?

(Jamie claps his hands together, loud.)

JAMIE: Just like that.

BEATRICE: ... Weird.

(Jamie moves around the room, trying to find Beatrice.)

JAMIE: It was totally weird. No warning. Because one second it was happening. It was music. And that light. And then nothing. Then just this.

BEATRICE: That music was awful.

JAMIE: I love that music.

BEATRICE: Why?

(Jamie stops.)

JAMIE: I don't know.

(Silence. Darkness.)

BEATRICE: Well, I guess that's it.

(Jamie starts moving again.)

JAMIE: Because there's not enough of it.

BEATRICE: Sorry?

JAMIE: It's good because there's not enough of it. It's great because of that ... Because it leaves spaces. And the spaces are incredible. Big, and full of nothing, and incredible. Because you can go wherever you want. In your head, you can just go. Just be somewhere else ... That's why I love the music.

(Beat.)

BEATRICE: I would like to go somewhere else. I think I would like that very much.

JAMIE: I have that music.

BEATRICE: Do you?

JAMIE: Yeah. I have tons of that music. A plethora. All kinds of spaces where you can go to all different kinds of places ... It's just on my iPod but you can ... We can share the headphones. One side each. We can do that ...

(Jamie stops.)

JAMIE: If you want.

(Beat.)

BEATRICE: Beatrice.

JAMIE: What?

(Beatrice walks to the door and stands in the light.)

BEATRICE: Beatrice.

(Beatrice opens the door.)

JAMIE: Okay ...

(Beatrice turns and exits through the door, leaving it open.)

JAMIE: ... Okay.

(Jamie runs after her. The door remains open.)

THE END.

NOTES

NOTES

NOTES

NOTES

www.ingramcontent.com/pod-product-compliance
Lightning Source LLC
Chambersburg PA
CBHW062023040426

42447CB00010B/2110